ISBN 978-0-265-08265-2
PIBN 10948056

1 MONTH OF
FREE
READING

at

www.ForgottenBooks.com

By purchasing this book you are eligible for one month membership to ForgottenBooks.com, giving you unlimited access to our entire collection of over 1,000,000 titles via our web site and mobile apps.

To claim your free month visit:

www.forgottenbooks.com/free948056

FOREIGN CROPS AND MARKETS.

ISSUED WEEKLY BY THE BUREAU OF AGRICULTURAL ECONOMICS, UNITED STATES DEPARTMENT OF AGRICULTURE, WASHINGTON, D.C.

VOLUME 11.   AUGUST 10, 1925.   NO. 6.

Feature of Issue: EUROPEAN CROPS AND MARKETS

C R O P   P R O S P E C T S

- - - - - - -

SMALL GRAINS

The Prairie Provinces of Canada have received beneficial
rains which have somewhat relieved the drought stricken areas, according to the Canadian Pacific Railway Report of July 27. There
are still numerous points, however, particularly in Saskatchewan,
which have need of further rainfall.

There has been little change in the European crop situation.
Conditions outside of Russia continue generally favorable except
in Great Britain. In Ireland conditions are reported to be promising. In the Scandinavian and Baltic countries conditions are also
favorable. The outlook for the wheat crop of Portugal is good. The
condition of cereal crops in Russia on July 15 was considerably better than at the same time last year. On the basis of this condition
report, production during the current year is forecast at 72 million
short tons of grain.

In Australia, light rains have fallen during the week and
the outlook for the coming season continues favorable. In Argentina
conditions are generally favorable with temperatures slightly below
normal. Seasonal dry weather has prevailed during the last few weeks
but the moisture supply is ample as a result of the unusually heavy
rains about a month ago.

C R O P   P R O S P E C T S - C O N T ' D.

- - - - - - -

SMALL GRAINS - CONT'D.

During the week estimates of Rumanian crops have been revised upward. The new estimates are included in the following summary table:

CEREAL CROPS - PRODUCTION

	1924	1925	Decrease from 1924	Increase over 1924
WHEAT	1,000 bushels	1,000 bushels	Per cent	Per cent
Total 15 countries	1,969,446	1,984,119		.7
Rumania	70,421	106,519		51.3
Morocco	23,884	19,584	18.0	
Egypt	34,186	36,633		7.2
Total 18 countries	2,097,937	2,146,855		2.3
Estimated world total excluding Russia	3,091,000			
RYE				
Total 10 countries	319,989	431,659		34.9
Rumania	5,963	7,086		18.8
Total 11 countries	325,952	438,745		34.6
Estimated world total excluding Russia	728,000			
BARLEY				
Total 14 countries	632,055	695,953		10.1
Rumania	30,759	45,975		49.5
Total 15 countries	662,814	741,928		11.9
Estimated world total excluding Russia	1,202,000			
OATS				
Total 10 countries	2,243,615	2,047,029	8.8	
Rumania	42,013	60,695		44.5
Total 11 countries	2,285,628	2,107,724	7.8	
CORN				
Total 2 countries	2,463,777	3,131,552		27.1

Compiled from official sources and International Institute of Agriculture unless otherwise noted.

CROP PROSPECTS - CONT'D.
- - - - - - - - -

CORN

The outlook for the European corn crop is favorable - See page 178.
- - - - - - - - -

RICE

Acreage and production estimates and condition reports on rice received so far are generally favorable for the rice harvest although with nothing to report for India the picture is only fragmentary. Incomplete reports on acreage for seven countries are about two per cent greater than for those countries last year. The condition of the rice plant in Japan proper indicates about an average crop, according to a cable from Consul Stewart at Tokyo. Production for Japan in 1924 amounted to 17,961 million pounds and the average for the past ten years to 18,100 million. In Chosen, the Consul says that favorable conditions have been prevailing generally although flood damage affected a small area. A crop of 4,700 million pounds of cleaned rice for Chosen is predicted compared with 4,156 million in 1924. The expected increase in the crop of Java and Madura previously reported helps to indicate a prospect so far for a fair supply of rice. No statement has come in for China more recent than that reporting damage in the vicinity of Waichow and Poklo.

RICE ACREAGE, 1924, 1925.

Country	1924	1925	Decrease from 1924	Increase over 1924
	1,000 acres:	1,000 acres:	Per cent	Per cent
Java & Madura, amount standing and harvested on April 30 .... a/	·7,781	7,885		1.3
United States	892	998		11.9
Indo-China b/				
Annam c/	964	944	2.1	
Cambodia d/	20	17	15.0	
Ceylon	800	800		
Formosa, first crop ... e/	579	596	.	2.9
Italy	340	346		1.8
Bulgaria	10	11		9.5
Total above countries	11,386	11,597		1.9

a/ Total area harvested in 1924 preliminary figure 8,577,000 acres.
b/ Total area for Indo-China in 1924 was estimated to be 11,500,000 acres.
c/ Rice of first six months.
d/ Dry season rice.
e/ Total acreage 1924 estimated at 1,310,200 acres.

CROP PROSPECTS - CONT'D.
- - - - - - - -

SUGAR

Reports received during the past week on both cane and beets
have continued to be favorable. A consular report for Costa Rico and
a trade report for Hawaii mention favorable weather in both regions.
The sugar cane crop of Brazil had received favorable rains about the
first part of July in the north and in Bahia, according to Consul
Donovan at Rio de Janeiro. Harvesting was beginning in the north and
was well under way in Minas Geraes, Sao Paulo and Rio de Janeiro.
Planting was in progress in Bahia and beginning in Parahyba and Pernambuco.

Trade reports on the European sugar beet areas indicate continued satisfactory progress. No revisions or new estimates have been received by the Department on the beet sugar area in European countries
for which the estimates previously received are summarized below.

EUROPEAN SUGAR BEETS, 1924 AND 1925

	1924	1925	Decrease from 1923-24	Increase over 1923-24
	1,000 acres	1,000 acres	Per cent	Per cent
Total 13 countries ..	4,344,488	4,530,100		4.5
Total Europe	5,190,149			

- - - - - - -

COTTON

The condition of the Egyptian cotton crop on August 1 is offi-
cially reported to be slightly better than on the same date last year but
still slightly below average, being listed at 98 per cent of the ten-year
average in 1925 and 97 per cent in 1924, according to a cabled report
from the International Institute of Agriculture. Trade reports of July
16 indicated that the formation of bolls was making good progress and
that the leaf worm was diminishing, the damage caused being insignifi-
cant, but that the pink worm was beginning to appear.

The monsoon in India made good progress through most of July and
conditions were generally satisfactory according to trade advices, although in portions of Berar, Khandesh and the Deccan more rain was needed.
At two meteorological stations the rainfall so far this season was considerably above the amount that had fallen up to the same date last
season.

CROP PROSPECTS - CONT'D.
- - - - - - -

Cotton acreage in the Gezira region of the Anglo-Egyptian Sudan for the current season is now estimated at 80,000 acres as compared with 20,000 acres planted in 1924 for the 1924-25 harvest, according to a cable from the International Institute of Agriculture, the big increase being mainly the result of the opening up of new areas through the completion of the Makwar dam.

The weather in Brazil during the latter part of June was generally favorable along the coast from Rio Grande do Sul to Alagoas, according to Consul Donovan at Rio de Janeiro. Frosts were reported in some areas away from the coastal zone. In the northwestern areas the lack of rain was favorable to the harvesting, which was in progress in Bahia, Piauhy, Para and Maramhao. The consul reports yields below normal in Sao Paulo and Minas Geraes.

COTTON: Acreage and production of the coming crop in countries reporting to date

Country	1924-25	1925-26	Decrease from 1924-25	Increase over 1924-25
	1,000 acres	1,000 acres	Per cent	Per cent
AREA -				
Total previously reported ..	44,140	48,190		9
Estimated world total	79,500			
	1,000 bales	1,000 bales	Per cent	Per cent
	478 lbs.net	478 lbs.net		
FORECASTS OF PRODUCTION -				
Total previously reported ..	14,150	14,419		
Estimated world total	24,700			

- - - - - - - -

FLAX

The Belgian crop on the whole is said by Consul Messersmith to have been in good condition through the first of July although in some regions of the country where the land was somewhat dry the length of the fiber was not satisfactory.

Consul Carlson at Kovno, Lithuania, reports that from the sown area of 151,966 acres for 1925 in that country an estimated production of 88,184,000 pounds of flax fiber is expected which would be an increase of 16,435,293 pounds over the last years official production estimate of 71,748,707 pounds.

CROP PROSPECTS - CONT'D.
- - - - - - - - -

The condition of the early sown flax crop of Ireland was promising through June according to Consul Brooks at Belfast, but the late sown fields had suffered from dry weather which checked the growth.

- - - - - -

TOBACCO

A decrease estimated at 40 to 50 per cent in the 1925 tobacco crop of the Remedios district of Cuba was reported by Consul Arthur C. Frost at Habana. The short crop was caused by a period of drought in the early part of the growing season. This statement is in line with a previous report for all of Cuba indicating a harvest 30 to 50 per cent less than last year.

Weather conditions for the tobacco crop of Brazil were favorable in Parahyba, Pernambuco and Bahia through early July. Harvesting is in progress in Minas Geraes, Goyaz, Sao Paulo and Bahia. Planting is in progress in Parahyba and Pernambuco according to Consul Howard Donovan at Rio de Janeiro.

Tobacco progress in Hungary which had been slow, showed rapid improvement during late June and early July due to beneficial rainfall, as reported by Consul Reneck at Budapest.

ONIONS

The yield of Egypt's onion crop was near normal, according to reports submitted near the end of harvesting.

FRUITS AND NUTS

The apple crop of England which was suffering from drought in the latter part of June and early July has been materially improved by recent ample rains, according to a cable received from Edwin Smith, Foreign Marketing Specialist. The trees started the season in good condition, with favorable weather during the blossoming period, according to official reports. Most varieties had a good show of bloom and were setting well. A lack of rain later, however, caused much dropping of the fruit. Disease and pests were reported to be causing damage in June.

CROP PROSPECTS - CONT'D.

- - - - - - - -

The present conditions of the 1925 fig crop in Smyrna as reported by the Trade Commissioner at Rome is not favorable due to extremely light precipitation during the winter and spring. This year's crop is expected to be twenty to twenty-five per cent below last year.

According to the trade Commissioner at Athens, the currant crop in Greece for 1924-25 is estimated at 337,989,080 pounds and the 1925-26 crop is expected to be 299,311,870 pounds, a decrease of about 39,000,000 pounds.

The Queen olives of the Seville consular district are somewhat damaged and the outlook is uncertain, according to a cable from Consul Burdett. The Manzanilla variety, however, is in good condition.

Correction.:- The statement in the issue of July 27, page 92 on the apple trees of Nova Scotia should be 100,000 apple trees have been set out in Nova Scotia this year instead of a 100 trees as given in the report.

MARKET NEWS AND PROSPECTS.

FIRMNESS CONTINUES IN FOREIGN BUTTER MARKETS.- With another week of slightly advancing prices on practically all descriptions of butter in London and in the official Copenhagen quotation, the market on August 7 was characterized as firm in the weekly cable from the American Agricultural Commissioner. The Copenhagen quotation was equivalent exactly to 92 score in New York at 43-1/2 cents, although the advance over last week from 410 kr. to 421 kr. is exaggerated somewhat by the rapidly rising exchange value of the Danish krone. In London Danish and Dutch were quoted at 44.8 cents and New Zealand at 42-1/2 cents. A detailed statement of prices in London, Copenhagen and New York appears on page 197.

GERMAN PORK MARKET EASIER.- Lard at Hamburg dropped 57 cents per 100 pounds to $20.00 for the week of August 5, according to W. A. Schoenfeld, Berlin Representative of the U. S. Department of Agriculture. The preceding week's quotation, which was the peak of the upward swing in progress during July, was the highest point reached during 1925. Hogs at Berlin were also easier at $18.04 per 100 pounds, with receipts of hogs at 14 markets totaling 52,527 for the week, an increase of nearly 20,000 over the preceding week and the highest number since the week of June 10. See page 197.

MARKET NEWS AND PROSPECTS, CONT'D.

PLENTIFUL SUPPLIES AND FIRM PRICES IN BRITISH PORK MARKETS.- Liverpool lard stocks at 15 million pounds on July 31 were nearly 3 million pounds greater than on June 30, 1925, and 84.6 per cent greater than on July 31, 19 according to cabled advices from E. A. Foley, American Agricultural Commiss at London. Lard stocks have been rising steadily since last February. Stoc of hams, bacon and shoulders totaled 13,851 boxes, a reduction below the June 30 figure of 727 boxes and of over 3,000 boxes below the figure of a year ago. July receipts of pork at London central markets reached 1,732,00C pounds, an increase of 95,000 pounds over the June figure.

For the week ending June 29, according to the Commissioner, Danish b prices in London reacted to $25.59 per 100 lbs., from their downward course the preceding four weeks. Canadian bacon rallied to $23.42. American bacon has not been quoted for the last four weeks. Supplies of hogs were heavier both England and Ireland, the former at 9,586, exceeding any week since June See Page 197.

AMERICAN WHEAT CANNOT COMPETE IN VIENNA.- For the first time this year American wheat cannot meet prices of Hungarian wheat in Vienna, accordi to cabled advices from G. C. Haas, American Agricultural Commissioner at Vie Hungarian wheat is now on an export basis and sells in Vienna at prices belo the world level. In Rumania and Yugoslavia wheat prices are too high to attempt exporting. Wheat prices in Vienna are expressive of crop prospects in the Danube basin and declined steadily during the week ended July 24. Wheat transactions are reported as small with buyers waiting for further price reductions.

HEAVY SALES OF MEXICAN SISAL.- July purchases of Mexican sisal total 140,000 bales, according to H. Vogenitz, American Consul at Progreso. Buyer paid 8 3/8 cents f.o.b. ships against 8 3/4 during June, planters receiving the old rate of 6 3/4 cents f.o.b. wharves. July shipments totaled 61,619 bales against 43,131 for June. American buyers took all of the June shipmer and 43,131 bales in July. Stocks on August 1 at Progreso reached 40,777 bal against 29,439 bales for July 1.

YUGOSLAVIA EXPECTS AN AVERAGE EXPORT OF PRUNES.- Yugoslavia will no export more than 44,000 short tons of prunes this season, according to recer cabled advices from G. C. Haas, American Agricultural Commissioner at Vienna This figure is the minimum of the possible exports of 44,000-50,000 short to reported earlier.

TIENTSIN DISTRICT MAY EXPORT MORE PEANUTS.- From 15,000 to 20,000 lor tons of peanuts in the shell will be available for export during the 1925-26 season if normal growing conditions prevail, according to Granville Woodard, American Vice Consul at Tientsin, China. The 1924-25 exports for 9 months amounted to about 9,000 long tons and in 1923-24 for 12 months, to 26,000 long tons. Tientsin is the leading source of Chinese peanuts for export in the shell.

F R U I T   N E W S

ISLE OF PINES WILL SHIP FEWER GRAPEFRUIT.- For the period August-June, 1925-26, the Isle of Pines expects to export about 175,000 cases of grapefruit to the United States, according to S. Talbott, American Vice Consul at Nueva Gerona. That figure would be a 20 per cent reduction below the exports for the same period of 1924-25. By months, the shipments will be: August 36,000 cases; September 72,000; October 48,000 and 18,000 cases for the other months. The first shipment is due in New York on August 18. The fruit is said to be large and good prices are expected.

PORTO RICO EXPECTS TO SHIP MORE GRAPEFRUIT AND PINEAPPLES.- Shipments of Porto Rico grapefruit for the year ending June 30, 1926 and expected to exceed the 580,000 boxes sent out during the preceding twelve months, according to H. C. Henricksen, of the Porto Rico Experiment Station. Pineappples are also expected to exceed the 343,000 boxes shipped last year. See page 189.

GRAPEFRUIT SELLS BRISKLY IN LONDON.- Demand for grapefruit is keener than ever in London, according to trade advices from E. A. Foley, American Agricultural Commissioner at London. The fruit is arriving sold, with dealers trying to meet advance orders, and serving customers in rotation as supplies are available.

ITALY WILL SEND FEWER LEMONS TO U.S. MARKETS.- California competition, the Tariff and fear of quarantines are killing Italian interest in the United States as a market for winter lemons, according to John Osborne, American Consul General at Genoa. Greater efforts are being made to regain the prewar Russian and German markets.

DOMESTIC APPLES ON BRITISH MARKETS.- British grown apples appeared in London this season in mid-July, according to trade notes from Edward A. Foley, American Agricultural Commissioner. They are showing signs of a dry season, and are recommended only for cooking purposes. Australian and New Zealand supplies, used as dessert fruit, are becoming dearer as their season approaches its close.

NETHERLANDS APPLE EXPORTS.- Exports of domestic apples from the Netherlands during 1924 amounted to 25,550 short tons compared with 18,470 tons during 1923, according to Consul J. S. Edwards at Amsterdam. Germany took 85 per cent of the exports as compared with only 45 per cent in 1923. Shipments to England and to Scandinavian countries show large decreases.

HEAVY APPLE CROP IN NOVA SCOTIA.- Prospects indicate an apple crop of 2-1/2 million barrels in the Annapolis Valley for 1925, according to B. Gottlieb, American Consul at Halifax. That figure is an increase of approximately 25 per cent over the 2 million barrel average of the last six years.

S U M M A R I E S   O F   L E A D I N G   A R T I C L E S
- - - - - - -

EUROPEAN WHEAT CROP AND MARKET PROSPECTS.- Indications point to a
European wheat crop for 1925, outside of Russia, larger than for 1924 and
about equal to that of 1923. Granted continued favorable conditions, Europe,
not including Russia, will produce from 150 to 200 million bushels more of
wheat and about 150 million bushels more of rye. Increased production, however, does not necessarily presage the diminishing of imports of wheat to a
corresponding degree. Experience has shown that Europeans consume wheat
readily when it is easily available, thereby maintaining imports even in
years of plentiful domestic production. Countries of normally small production, such as Great Britain show no great variation at any time in the amounts
imported.

In the Danube Basin, always an important source of supply for wheat
in Europe, the aggregate production in Rumania, Bulgaria and Hungary this
year is estimated at 213 million bushels against 150 million bushels for 1924.
Bulgaria may export from 5 to 10 million bushels and Hungary, about 10 million
bushels. The Rumanian export is still problematical. These sources of supply, particularly Rumania, are subject to governmental regulations which tend
to render exports irregular. G. C. Haas, American Agricultural Commissioner
at Vienna, reports that Rumanian wheat prices have tended to be higher than
the world price level, and that until recently, United States wheat has com-
peted with the Hungarian grain in the Vienna market. The Vienna market, according to Mr. Haas, reflects rather accurately conditions in the Chicago
market, and also acts as a good index of the Danube price situation. Low
stocks in that area, in common with Europe generally, have tended to main-
tain price levels. Buyers have been avoiding future commitments in anticipa-
tion of more definite news as to the world crop for 1925.

Russia is expected to make some contribution this season to the grain
supply of western Europe. North Africa also promises more severe competition
with our Durum wheats in the Mediterranean countries. With the outlook in
Europe more favorable from the production standpoint, therefore, it is evident that, while European countries will probably import not quite as much
wheat as in a less plentiful year, competition on those markets among non-
European producers will be keener than it was last season.   See page 171.

BETTER ECONOMIC SITUATION IN EUROPE: European postwar economic recovery, while slow is none the less definite. The outstanding manifestation of
that recovery is an increased purchasing power. As far as the consumption
of agricultural products is concerned, however, the results of that increased
purchasing power will be seen rather in demand for better quality products
than for greatly increased quantities. Staple agricultural goods were imported even at periods of extreme depression in quantities sufficient to meet
domestic requirements. While some increased demand for staples may occur,
no phenomenal increase is expected to accompany the present gradual return
to economic stability. See page 185.

THE EUROPEAN WHEAT CROP AND MARKET PROSPECTS

Estimates and forecasts of production in 9 European countries reported to date indicate a production of 627 million bushels of wheat, as compared with 483 million bushels last year and 648 million bushels in 1923. The same countries report 372 million bushels of rye compared with 249 million bushels last year and 359 million in 1923. These 9 countries account for only about one-half of the wheat and rye crops of Europe outside of Russia. Countries which have not yet estimated production, report generally favorable conditions with the exception of Great Britain. In Great Britain recent improvement is reported but yields are expected to be rather poor. In Ireland, however, conditions are promising. In France, Germany, Yugoslavia and Czechoslovakia conditions are favorable and yields well above average are indicated. In Greece a harvest 70 per cent above last year is promised. Conditions in Portugal are good. In the Scandinavian and Baltic countries conditions are promising. A crop considerably larger than last year and about equal to the crop of 1923 is indicated for all of Europe outside of Russia. Should these indications be borne out, Europe will have, outside of Russia, from 150 to 200 million bushels more of wheat and about 150 million bushels more of rye than she had last year.

It is not to be expected, however, that the European demand for wheat and rye from other countries will be reduced in comparison with last year by as much as the increase in production. Following the large crop of 1923, the net imports of wheat and flour amounted to 554 million bushels. The reduction of 200 million bushels of wheat and nearly 175 million bushels of rye in the crop of 1924 caused an increase in the imports of wheat of only about 75 million bushels.

In many of the countries which produce large quantities of wheat and rye, such as France, Spain, Italy and Germany, there is a tendency for the utilization or consumption of wheat to vary with production. This fact is shown clearly in the Wheat Studies of the Food Research Institute (See Vol.1, No. 7 June, 1925). In 1923 these countries imported more wheat than they were expected to import, not only because wheat was cheap but also because wheat being more plentiful on the farms and at interior consuming centers, more was consumed than would have been consumed even at the low prices had the world supplies been large and the domestic supplies small. On the other hand when crops are short they conserve their home supplies and do not import enough to make up the deficit in crop production.

In some of the smaller countries, such as Switzerland, Belgium, Denmark and Netherlands, imports may vary with production but the total of imports of these is not very large and production is small and therefore does not vary greatly in quantity. The United Kingdom, the greatest European importer, produces such a small part of her consumption that the variations in her crops have little effect upon her imports.

THE EUROPEAN WHEAT CROP AND MARKET PROSPECTS,-CONT'D.

The countries of the Danube basin are an important factor in the Europea wheat situation. Some of the Danube countries will have grain for export. Rumania, Bulgaria, and Hungary report considerable increases this year over last. The indicated production in these 3 countries amounts to 213 million bushels as compared with 150 million bushels last year.

WHEAT: Danubian Countries, Acreage, Average 1909-13 Annual 1920 to 1925

Country	Average 1909-13 Present Boundaries	1920	1921	1922	1923	1924	1925
	1,000 acres	1,000 acres	1,000 acres	1,000 acres	1,000 acres	1,000 acres	1,000 acres
Austria........:	635:a/	371:a/	378:a/	460:	475:	482:b/	(1
Czechoslovakia.:	1,718:	1,566:	1,566:	1,675:	1,507:	1,497:	1,5
Hungary........:	3,712:	2,672:	2,388:	3,522:	3,320:	3,499:	3,6
Yugoslavia.....:	3,982:	3,550:	3,687:	3,673:	3,843:	4,244:	4,6
Bulgaria.......:	2,409:	2,183:	2,233:	2,226:	2,303:	2,462:	2,5
Rumania........:c/	9,515:	4,998:	6,149:	6,547:	6,648:	7,839:	7,6
Total......:	21,971:	15,340:	16,891:	18,103:	18,096:	20,023:	20,0
Per cent of 1909-13.....:		69.8	76.9:	82.4:	82.4:	91.1:	9

a/ Territory not quite comparable with other years.
b/ Figures for previous year brought forward.
c/ Four year average.

WHEAT: Danubian Countries, Production,Average 1909-13 Annual 1920 to 1925

Country	Average 1909-13 Present boundaries	1920	1921	1922	1923	1924	192
	1,000 bushels	1,000 bushels	1,000 bushels	1,000 bushels	1,000 bushels	1,000 bushels	1,00 bushe
Austria........:	12,813	a/ 5,434:a/	6,530:a/	7,422:	8,889:	8,490:	
Czechoslovakia.:	37,879	26,436:	38,682:	33,621:	36,226:	32,238:	
Hungary........:	71,493	38,294:	52,715:	54,729:	67,705:	51,568:	63,
Yugoslavia.....:	62,024	43,011:	51,809:	44,472:	61,069:	57,771:	
Bulgaria.......:	37,823	30,003:	29,239:	37,704:	36,223:	28,317:	43,
Rumania........:b/	158,672	61,309:	78,563:	92,007:	102,311:	70,421:	106,
Total......:	380,704:	204,487:	257,538:	269,955:	312,423:	248,805:	
Per cent of 1909-13......:		53.7	67.6	70.9	82.1	65.4	

a/ Territory not quite comparable with other years.
b/ Four year average.

THE EUROPEAN WHEAT CROP AND MARKET PROSPECTS, CONT'D.

Bulgaria is harvesting a record crop. Wheat production in that country has recovered from the effects of the war. The area harvested, which was reduced from 2,400,000 acres, the average before the war, to 2,200,000 acres in 1920, has now reached 2,500,000 acres. The 1925 crop is estimated to be nearly 44 million bushels, as compared with a pre-war average of 38 million bushels. From this crop Bulgaria can export from 5 to 10 million bushels.

Hungarian wheat production in present territory has almost recovered from the effects of the war, the area having reached 3,600,000 acres as compared with 2,700,000 in 1920 and 3,700,000 before the war. The indicated production for this year is about 63 million bushels, as compared with 52 million last year and 71 million before the war. From this crop Hungary may export about 10 million bushels.

Rumania has made less progress. The wheat production in Rumania is still far below pre-war production in the same area. The area for wheat in Rumania is estimated to be 7,800,000 acres, as compared with 5,000,000 in 1920 and 9,500,000 before the war. Production in 1925 is estimated to be nearly 107 million bushels as compared with 70 million bushels last year and 159 million before the war.

The amount of wheat that Rumania will export this year is problematical. Agricultural Commissioner Haas reports that it is unofficially estimated that the exports of wheat will amount to 37 million bushels, but this is probably too high a figure. He says further: "An important point to be considered in forming an estimate of the grain export from Rumania is what export policy the Rumanian Government will adopt. At present considerable dissatisfaction is expressed in Rumania against the Government's policy concerning the grain export. In June at a Congress of the Rumanian Agricultural associations a resolution was adopted petitioning the Government to allow free export of grains and to abolish the system of fixed and maximum prices for grain, maintaining that this policy did not cheapen the cost of living but only reduced the areas planted to wheat. In the fall of 1924 when there was a rapid increase in the world market prices for wheat, the Government found it necessary because of the small crop to hold down the export by increasing the export duty on wheat. It was expected that this would make the export unprofitable and the inland price of wheat would decrease by the amount of the increase of the export duty. However, as it actually worked out no wheat was available at these low prices and the peasants held back their grain until the mills agreed to pay considerably higher prices. The increase of prices continued during the spring months of 1925 when an export prohibition was ordered. But in spite of the export prohibition, Rumanian wheat prices were sometimes above the world level.

THE EUROPEAN WHEAT CROP AND MARKET PROSPECTS, CONT'D.

"The export prohibition has now been removed but it does not seem probable that the Rumanian Government will consent to a free trade in grain. In the first place the Government needs the revenue which it derives from the export tax and in the second place if the wheat market is good in the summer and autumn months this year, Rumanian circles fear that the peasants will bring large quantities of grain on the market which will be exported, as the mills, because of the high interest rates, will purchase only the amounts needed for current requirements. The country, they say, will then have sold all it's stocks and in spite of the good crop will again be in the same position as it was last year.

"According to a recent press report free trade is not to be permitted and the export of grain is to be subject to a new export tax."

Taking all of the Danube countries together including Austria and Czechoslovakia, the total wheat area in 1925 is about 91 per cent of the prewar average in the same territory. Official production estimates are available for only 3 of the 6 countries. According to private estimates, the yield of wheat in Yugoslavia may be 20 per cent larger than last year and the quality of it will be better than last year. Private reports also indicate that the grain crops in Czechoslovakia will be above average and in Austria slightly larger than last year. It seems probable that the production for these countries will be at least as great as it was in 1923, in which year it was 82 per cent of the pre-war average.

The current situation as to the grain market is reported by Agricultural Commissioner Haas, at Vienna, as follows:

"Business on the grain markets is reduced to a minimum, waiting more definite information concerning the new world crop. Since June 1, there has been practically no business in wheat on the Vienna Exchange, only nominal prices have been quoted. There was a little more business on the Budapest exchange but the prices are similar to those quoted in Vienna. Purchases are made only to cover the necessary immediate requirements. In spite of the favorable reports concerning the new crop in this area, the prices have remained fairly steady. The unfavorable reports from the United States, which indicates a better export outlook for this area, and the very low stocks of the old crop coupled with the fact that the new crop because of the recent wet weather, will have to be dried for a time before it is fit for milling, are factors in holding up the market.

"The prices in this area fluctuate in a general way with the prices on the American markets. The local exchanges watch Chicago prices closely. A grain market review in a Budapest paper remarks, 'Chicago is the only market expressing the international grain situation. All other markets exhibit a more or less local colour'.

THE EUROPEAN WHEAT CROP AND MARKET PROSPECTS - CONT'D.

... "Prices of wheat on the Vienna exchange, which are a good index of
Danube price situation, are given in the accompanying table in comparison
1 the New York prices and the cost of transporting grain from New York
Vienna. When differences in quality are considered American wheat
been   on a competing basis with the local wheat.

WHEAT PRICES AT NEW YORK AND VIENNA, WEEKLY, APRIL 12 -
JUNE 13, 1925.

Date	Price per bushel, New York	Freight to Triest per bushel	Freight to Vienna and other, expenses	Total cost at Vienna	Domestic wheat price Vienna
	Cents	Cents	Cents per bu.	Cents per bu.	Cents per bu.
il 12-18...:	164.7	8.3	12.6	185.6	196.7
19-25...:	164.5	8.3	12.6	185.5	199.0
26-May 2..:	166.3	8.3	12.6	187.2	200.9
3-9......:	177.4	9.0	12.6	198.9	201.4
10-16....:	177.9	9.6	12.6	200.0	204.7
17-23.....:	179.8	10.1	12.4	202.4	204.7
24-30......:	186.1	10.1	12.2	208.5	199.0
31-June 6..:	183.1	7.8	12.3	203.2	199.0
e 7-13....:	181.0	5.4	12.2	198.6	199.0
14-20.....:					199.0
21-27.....:					199.0
28-July 4..:					199.0
y 5-11....:					199.0

"In Hungary, stocks of the old crop are reported by the trade to be very
11. Business is very slack. The market is in a formative mood waiting
more definite information concerning the new world crop situation. Milling
at a standstill. The higher developed Hungarian milling industry, which is too
ge for the present territory of Hungary, is suffering in consequence of the
tective duties in force in the neighboring countries and of the lack of
mercial treaties. All of the large mills are obliged to export their products,
the inland consumption with the exception of Budapest is supplied by small
al mills. The mills which were formerly in Hungarian territory but now are
ated in Yugoslavia are suffering under similar conditions."

"Stocks of wheat and flour are exhausted. Wheat and wheat flour are now
ng imported. It is reported that last year, owing to the lack of reliable
tistics the crop was overestimated and in consequence of this mistake,
export was forced by offering grain at very low prices so as to insure a
ll carryover into the new harvesting period. As a consequence too much
at was exported early and until the new crop arrives, wheat must be im-
ted at high prices. The mills are buying only to cover the necessary immediate
quirements. Mills which are operating are using imported Hungarian and American

THE EUROPEAN WHEAT CROP AND MARKET PROSPECTS, CONT'D.

"The export prohibition has now been removed but it does not seem pro
bable that the Rumanian Government will consent to a free trade in grain.
In the first place the Government needs the revenue which it derives from
the export tax and in the second place if the wheat market is good in the
summer and autumn months this year, Rumanian circles fear that the peasants
will bring large quantities of grain on the market which will be exported, a
the mills, because of the high interest rates, will purchase only the amount
needed for current requirements. The country, they say, will then have sold
all it's stocks and in spite of the good crop will again be in the same posi
as it was last year.

"According to a recent press report free trade is not to be permitted
and the export of grain is to be subject to a new export tax."

Taking all of the Danube countries together including Austria and
Czechoslovakia, the total wheat area in 1925 is about 91 per cent of the pre
war average in the same territory. Official production estimates are availa
for only 3 of the 6 countries. According to private estimates, the yield of
wheat in Yugoslavia may be 20 per cent larger than last year and the quality
of it will be better than last year. Private reports also indicate that the
grain crops in Czechoslovakia will be above average and in Austria slightly
larger than last year. It seems probable that the production for these
countries will be at least as great as it was in 1923, in which year it was
82 per cent of the pre-war average.

The current situation as to the grain market is reported by Agricult
Commissioner Haas, at Vienna, as follows:

"Business on the grain markets is reduced to a minimum, waiting more
definite information concerning the new world crop. Since June 1, there ha
been practically no business in wheat on the Vienna Exchange, only nominal
prices have been quoted. There was a little more business on the Budapest
exchange but the prices are similar to those quoted in Vienna. Purchases a
made only to cover the necessary immediate requirements. In spite of the f
able reports concerning the new crop in this area, the prices have remained
fairly steady. The unfavorable reports from the United States, which indic
a better export outlook for this area, and the very low stocks of the old
crop coupled with the fact that the new crop because of the recent wet weat
will have to be dried for a time before it is fit for milling, are factors
in holding up the market.

"The prices in this area fluctuate in a general way with the prices
the American markets. The local exchanges watch Chicago prices closely. A
grain market review in a Budapest paper remarks, 'Chicago is the only marke
expressing the international grain situation. All other markets exhibit a
or less local colour'.

THE EUROPEAN WHEAT CROP AND MARKET PROSPECTS - CONT'D.

"Prices of wheat on the Vienna exchange, which are a good index of
the Danube price situation, are given in the accompanying table in comparison
with the New York prices and the cost of transporting grain from New York
to Vienna. When differences in quality are considered American wheat
has been   on a competing basis with the local wheat.

WHEAT PRICES AT NEW YORK AND VIENNA, WEEKLY, APRIL 12 -
JUNE 13, 1925.

Date	Price per bushel, New York	Freight to Triest per bushel	Freight to Vienna and other expenses	Total cost at Vienna	Domestic wheat price Vienna
	Cents	Cents	Cents per bu.	Cents per bu.	Cents per bu.
April 12-18...	164.7	8.3	12.6	185.6	196.7
" 19-25...	164.5	8.3	12.6	185.5	199.0
" 26-May 2...	166.3	8.3	12.6	187.2	200.9
May 3-9.......	177.4	9.0	12.6	198.9	201.4
" 10-16......	177.9	9.6	12.6	200.0	204.7
" 17-23......	179.8	0.1	12.4	202.4	204.7
" 24-30......	186.1	10.1	12.2	208.5	199.0
" 31-June 6...	183.1	7.8	12.3	203.2	199.0
June 7-13.....	181.0	5.4	12.2	198.6	199.0
" 14-20.....					199.0
" 21-27.....					199.0
" 28-July 4...					199.0
July 5-11.....					199.0

"In Hungary, stocks of the old crop are reported by the trade to be very
small. Business is very slack. The market is in a formative mood waiting
for more definite information concerning the new world crop situation. Milling
is at a standstill. The higher developed Hungarian milling industry, which is too
large for the present territory of Hungary, is suffering in consequence of the
protective duties in force in the neighboring countries and of the lack of
commercial treaties. All of the large mills are obliged to export their products,
as the inland consumption with the exception of Budapest is supplied by small
local mills. The mills which were formerly in Hungarian territory but now are
located in Yugoslavia are suffering under similar conditions."

"Stocks of wheat and flour are exhausted. Wheat and wheat flour are now
being imported. It is reported that last year, owing to the lack of reliable
statistics the crop was overestimated and in consequence of this mistake,
the export was forced by offering grain at very low prices so as to insure a
small carryover into the new harvesting period. As a consequence too much
wheat was exported early and until the new crop arrives, wheat must be imported at high prices. The mills are buying only to cover the necessary immediate
requirements. Mills which are operating are using imported Hungarian and American

THE EUROPEAN WHEAT CROP AND MARKET PROSPECTS - CONT'D.

wheat. Business in the old wheat is entirely at a standstill as all the reserves are used up. Mills for the most part are idle and are repairing their machinery for the new milling period."

From the above analysis of the situation in the countries of the Danube Basin, it is evident that the absence of stocks of old wheat is a strengthening factor in the European wheat markets at the beginning of the season. If the latest information as to probable production is borne out, on the other hand, the net imports of these Danube countries as a group will be considerably less than last year, with the possibility of a small balance for contribution to the needs of other European countries.

The condition of cereal crops in Russia on July 15 was considerably better than at the same time last year according to a cablegram from the international Institute of Agriculture. On the basis of this condition the cable states that the production of cereals is estimated at about 72 million short tons or an increase of 18 million tons compared with last year. Although it is impossible to estimate the probable exports of wheat and rye from Russia on the basis of available reports, that country probably will contribute something to the needs of the Western European countries. Exports from Russia together with exports from Northern Africa promise us greater competition than last year with our Durum wheat in the markets in the Mediterranean Basin.

GOOD EUROPEAN CORN OUTLOOK WITH SURPLUS IN DANUBE COUNTRIES

The outlook for the European corn crop is favorable. Estimates of acreage from six countries reporting give a total of 15,757,000 acres against 15,459,000 acres for the same countries last year, an increase of about 1.9 per cent, and represents more than half of the total European acreage. Data are still lacking, however, for such large producers as Spain, Hungary, Yugoslavia and Russia. France is the only country reporting a decrease, the 1925 estimate being 701,000 acres against a harvested area of 846,000 acres in 1924. Italy reports a slight increase. In both France and Italy, crop conditions indicate yields above average.

In the Lower Danube area, the European surplus producing region, conditions are promising. Rumania, Europe's largest producer, reports a considerable increase in acreage with the crop well advanced and making rapid progress. The Bulgarian crop is forecast at 36 million bushels against 27 million bushels last year. No production forecasts are yet available for Hungary or Yugoslavia, but condition reports indicate yields above average.

Fairly large stocks of corn exist in the Danube basin, according to United States Agricultural Commissioner Haas at Vienna. In Yugoslavia on June 19, it was unofficially estimated that about 8 million bushels of corn of the 1924 crop were destined for export with a considerable carryover remaining. Trade in domestic corn in those countries is suffering from competition from Argentina. It seems likely that there must be a considerable reduction of prices if the corn now remaining in the Danube region is to be marketed.

RUSSIAN AGRICULTURAL EXPORTS

October 1924 - March 1925.

The value of agricultural exports from the Soviet Union in the first
if the fiscal year beginning October 1, 1924, was only 13.4 per cent
the value in the corresponding period of the previous year, in spite
: sharp curtailment of grain exports, according to the "Russian Review".

Exports of all grains, seeds and oil cake in the period under review
:ated as amounting to 556,841 short tons as compared with 2,132,569 short
in the corresponding period of 1923-24. Figures of exports of individual
lities are incomplete, but such data as are available indicate that less
200,000 tons of all grains were exported from Russia in the six months
g March 31. These exports were probably largely corn and barley, and
more than counterbalanced in value by the imports of wheat and flour in
atter part of the season. Over 200,000 short tons of oil cake and over
00, tons of seed were exported during this period. Exports of oil cake
eeds were greater than in the same six months of the previous season.

Exports of flax and tow during these months were more than double those
e corresponding period a year ago, amounting to 111,000,000 pounds.
r products exports remained about stationary. Exports of bristles increas-
om 758,000 pounds to 1,878,000 lbs. Butter exports declined from 5,706,000
to 4,367,000 lbs. while exports of eggs increased from 3,833,000 dozen
,750,000 dozen.

Imports of agricultural products into the Soviet Union for the six months
g March 31, 1925 are stated as follows in short tons, wheat, 15,619;
, 67,431; tea, 2,504; sugar, 83,004; cotton, 24,724 and wool, 3,518.

The destinations of agricultural exports from the Soviet Union are not
ately stated, but of all exports 30 per cent go to the United Kingdom,
r cent to Lativia, probably largely for reexport, 16 per cent to Germany,
' cent to the United States and 32 per cent to other countries. Of the
. imports, 23 per cent originate in the United Kingdom, 19 per cent in
inited States, 17 per cent in Germany and 41 per cent in other countries.

Russian Cotton Purchases.

The All-Russian Textile Syndicate, Inc., which purchases cotton for
.an mills has just completed its purchases in the United States from the
of the past season, according to the Russian Review.

The total purchases amounted to 243,698 bales valued at $36,340,000 c.i.f.
insk, the port on the Arctic Ocean to which all cotton shipments on account
ie syndicate are consigned. Over 195,000 bales had been shipped up to June 30,
five additional cargoes with a total of 48,000 bales scheduled to sail from
ports in July.

Purchases of cotton in the United States by this Syndicate from the crop of
-24 amounted to 189,145 bales, making a total of 432,843 bales purchased since
irganization of the syndicate.

wheat. Business in the old wheat is entirely at a standstill as all the res
are used up. Mills for the most part are idle and are repairing their machi
ery for the new milling period."

From the above analysis of the situation in the countries of the Danu
Basin, it is evident that the absence of stocks of old wheat is a strengthen
factor in the European wheat markets at the beginning of the season. If the
latest information as to probable production is borne out, on the other hand
the net imports of these Danube countries as a group will be considerably le
than last year, with the possibility of a small balance for contribution to
the needs of other European countries.

The condition of cereal crops in Russia on July 15 was considerably
better than at the same time last year according to a cablegram from the int
national Institute of Agriculture. On the basis of this condition the cable
states that the production of cereals is estimated at about 72 million short
tons or an increase of 18 million tons compared with last year. Although it
is impossible to estimate the probable exports of wheat and rye from Russia
on the basis of available reports, that country probably will contribute som
thing to the needs of the Western European countries. Exports from Russia
together with exports from Northern Africa promise us greater competition th
last year with our Durum wheat in the markets in the Mediterranean Basin.

GOOD EUROPEAN CORN OUTLOOK WITH SURPLUS IN DANUBE COUNTRIES

The outlook for the European corn crop is favorable. Estimates of
acreage from six countries reporting give a total of 15,757,000 acres agains
15,459,000 acres for the same countries last year, an increase of about 1.9
per cent, and represents more than half of the total European acreage. Dat
are still lacking, however, for such large producers as Spain, Hungary, Yug
slavia and Russia. France is the only country reporting a decrease, the 19
estimate being 701,000 acres against a harvested area of 846,000 acres in 1
Italy reports a slight increase. In both France and Italy, crop conditions
indicate yields above average.

In the Lower Danube area, the European surplus producing region, con
are promising. Rumania, Europe's largest producer, reports a considerable
in acreage with the crop well advanced and making rapid progress. The Bulg
crop is forecast at 36 million bushels against 27 million bushels last year
No production forecasts are yet available for Hungary or Yugoslavia, but co
dition reports indicate yields above average.

Fairly large stocks of corn exist in the Danube basin, according to
States Agricultural Commissioner Haas at Vienna. In Yugoslavia on June 19,
was unofficially estimated that about 8 million bushels of corn of the 1924
were destined for export with a considerable carryover remaining. Trade in
domestic corn in those countries is suffering from competition from Argent
It seems likely that there must be a considerable reduction of prices if the
corn now remaining in the Danube region is to be marketed.

RUSSIAN AGRICULTURAL EXPORTS

October 1924 - March 1925.

The value of agricultural exports from the Soviet Union in the first half of the fiscal year beginning October 1, 1924, was only 13.4 per cent below the value in the corresponding period of the previous year, in spite of the sharp curtailment of grain exports, according to the "Russian Review".

Exports of all grains, seeds and oil cake in the period under review are stated as amounting to 556,841 short tons as compared with 2,132,569 short tons in the corresponding period of 1923-24. Figures of exports of individual commodities are incomplete, but such data as are available indicate that less than 200,000 tons of all grains were exported from Russia in the six months ending March 31. These exports were probably largely corn and barley, and were more than counterbalanced in value by the imports of wheat and flour in the latter part of the season. Over 200,000 short tons of oil cake and over 150,000, tons of seed were exported during this period. Exports of oil cake and seeds were greater than in the same six months of the previous season.

Exports of flax and tow during these months were more than double those of the corresponding period a year ago, amounting to 111,000,000 pounds. Timber products exports remained about stationary. Exports of bristles increased from 758,000 pounds to 1,878,000 lbs. Butter exports declined from 5,706,000 lbs. to 4,367,000 lbs. while exports of eggs increased from 3,833,000 dozen to 16,750,000 dozen.

Imports of agricultural products into the Soviet Union for the six months ending March 31, 1925 are stated as follows in short tons, wheat, 15,619; flour, 67,431; tea, 2,504; sugar, 83,004; cotton, 24,724 and wool, 3,518.

The destinations of agricultural exports from the Soviet Union are not separately stated, but of all exports 30 per cent go to the United Kingdom, 18 per cent to Latvia, probably largely for reexport, 16 per cent to Germany, 4 per cent to the United States and 32 per cent to other countries. Of the total imports, 23 per cent originate in the United Kingdom, 19 per cent in the United States, 17 per cent in Germany and 41 per cent in other countries.

Russian Cotton Purchases.

The All-Russian Textile Syndicate, Inc., which purchases cotton for Russian mills has just completed its purchases in the United States from the crop of the past season, according to the Russian Review.

The total purchases amounted to 243,698 bales valued at $36,340,000 c.i.f. Murmansk, the port on the Arctic Ocean to which all cotton shipments on account of the syndicate are consigned. Over 195,000 bales had been shipped up to June 30, with five additional cargoes with a total of 48,000 bales scheduled to sail from Gulf ports in July.

Purchases of cotton in the United States by this Syndicate from the crop of 1923-24 amounted to 189,145 bales, making a total of 432,843 bales purchased since the organization of the syndicate.

BRITISH FOOD PRICES AT HIGHER LEVELS

Prices of agricultural products in Great Britain have recently show a tendency to increase. The general average for the period January-April 1925 was above that of the same period of 1924. With the annual average of 1911-13 as a base, the percentage increases of agricultural prices for the past few years are as follows:

Year	:	Per Cent	:	Year	:	Per Cent
1920............:	:	192	:	1923.....:	:	57
1921............:	:	119	:	1924.....:	:	61
1922............:	:	69	:		:	

During 1924 British farmers furnished most of the potatoes and oats consumed in that country; about 1/2 of the barley and eggs; less than 1/2 of the meat and fruit; about 1/3 of the cheese; less than 1/5 of the wheat and butter and 1/10 of the wool. The following table gives the percentages of the total supply of the principal agricultural commodities in the United Kingdom as drawn from various sources during 1924:

BRITISH FOOD SUPPLY: Home Production During
1924 in Relation to Total Supply

Commodity	Home Produced	Imported From		
		Irish Free State	British Possessions	Foreign Countries
	Per Cent	Per Cent	Per Cent	Per Cent
Wheat a/	18	(c)	43	39
Barley	51	(c)	21	28
Oats	83	1	5	11
Beef and Veal b/	44	6	7	43
Mutton & Lamb b/	41	2	31	26
Pig-meat b/	34	8	7	51
Butter	17	7	30	46
Cheese	31	(c)	60	9
Eggs	50	11	2	37
Potatoes	92	(c)	1	7
Wool	10	2	71	17
Fruit d/	44	(c)	16	40

Source: British Ministry of Agriculture and Fisheries.
a/ Including flour expressed as wheat. b/ Meat statistics refer to 12 months ended May, 1924. c/ Less than 1/2 per cent. d/ Total of apples, cherries, currants, gooseberries, pears, plums, and strawberries.

INCREASED PURCHASING POWER AND MEAT CONSUMPTION IN GERMANY

A comparison of livestock prices and marketings in Germany in the first four months of 1925 as compared with the same months of 1924 indicates a very distinct increase in the purchasing power of the German people, although this purchasing power has not yet reached the pre-war level, according to Dr. E. von der Warth, of the German Meat Importers Association. The following table shows the per cent of increase or decrease in prices of the various grades of livestock this year over last; as shown by reports from the 18 most important slaughter houses in Prussia.

Type of Animal	Grade	Price Change Per Cent	Marketings Per cent of Change
Steers	a	+13.3)	
	b	+12.0)	+25.6
	c	+12.9)	
	d	+11.7)	
Bulls	a	+16.2)	
	b	+18.1)	+16.4
	c	+20.4)	
Cows and heifers	a	+14.8)	
	b	+10.1)	
	c	+10.5)	+11.7
	d	+ 8.7)	
	e	+ 4.6)	
Feeders		+13.6)	+ 4.2
Calves	a	+13.4)	
	b	+13.3)	
	c	+16.8)	+20.1
	d	+18.6)	
	e	+17.3)	
Hogs	a	+ 2.4)	
	b	+ 2.3)	
	c	+ 2.5)	+31.2
	d	+ 3.6)	
	e	+ 7.5)	
	f	+ 0.3)	
Sheep, stall fed	a	+ 1.4)	
	b	- 3.6)	
	c	-10.5)	+67.2
Sheep, pasture fed	a	+ 7.8)	
	b	- 0)	

PURCHASING POWER AND MEAT CONSUMPTION IN GERMANY, CONT'D.

It will be noted that in spite of the greater numbers of animals marketed there have been increases in prices, especially in the case of cattle and calves. Furthermore, the better grades of animals have shown a relatively greater price advance and greater increases in marketing than the poorer grades. In the case of hogs and sheep marketings have shown a still heavier increase but prices have still shown some advance in all grades of hogs and for the best grades of sheep.

The total importation of all kinds of meats has increased from 130 million pounds in the first quarter of 1924 to 148 million in the same period of 1925. Here also the demand for better qualities of meats has manifested itself. For example, the imports of corned beef have dropped from 21 million lbs. in 1924 to 2 million in 1925, while the imports of fresh beef have increased from 441,000 lbs. in 1924 to 20,500,000 lbs. in 1925. Similarly the imports of frozen and pickled pork and bacon have dropped from 80 million to 56 million lbs. while the imports of fresh pork and live hogs have increased from 18 million lbs. to 56 million lbs. The increased imports of meat, however, have been more than counterbalanced by the decrease in imports of animal fats, which have declined from 120 million in the first four months of 1924 to 98 million lbs. in the same months of 1925. The combined importation of livestock, meats and animal fats was 259 million lbs. in the months Jan. - Mar. 1924, as compared with 246 million lbs in Jan. - Mar. 1925, a decline of about 5 per cent. One explanation of the decreased importation of animal fats is seen in the increase in butter imports in the same period from 13,250,000 lbs. in 1924 to 45 million lbs. in 1925. Similarly increases are shown in imports of cheese from 17 million lbs. in 1924 to nearly 33 million lbs. in 1925, and in eggs, from 21 million lbs. in 1924 to nearly 53 million lbs. in 1925. Milk imports have remained practically stationary.

While the indicated consumption of meats and dairy products shows a distinct improvement over last year, both in quantity and quality, it is to be noted that this years indicated consumption of meat and animal fats is still fully 17 per cent below the indicated consumption before the war, and that the consumption of dairy products is also much lower than before the war.

Dr. von der Warth states that greatly lessened domestic slaughterings with correspondingly higher prices are to be expected in the future. It is also likely that the imports of freshly slaughtered hogs from Poland, which amounted to nearly 90 million pounds during the six months ending May, 1925 will be almost completely cut off in the summer months by the new regulations requiring the importation of the viscera in the natural state with the carcasses. Considering all these factors, there seems to be a probability in the opinion of Dr. van der Warth, that meat consumption will decrease somewhat in future months.

HOGS AND PORK PRODUCTS: INDICES OF FOREIGN SUPPLIES, DEMAND AND PRICE

untry and Item	Unit	May 1909-13 Average	June 1909-13 Average	June 1924	May 1925	June 1925
d Kingdom:						
duction -						
Fat pigs at representative English markets.	Thousands			30	50	40
Pigs bought for curing in Ireland	"	a/ 101	a/ 93	83	71	67
Supplies of Brit. & Irish pork at London Central Markets......	Thousand pounds			1,669	1,745	1,637
ade -						
Imports -						
Ham and bacon.......	"	51,396	50,914	85,596	66,320	85,832
Lard	"	16,799	18,741	21,935	27,801	27,577
Exports -						
Bacon, hams & shoulders from U.S. to U.K. b/	"	24,045	24,220	31,582	23,112	29,230
Lard from U.S. to U.K. b/	"	16,876	16,030	17,826	29,484	21,930
ocks -						
Hams, bacon & shoulders: Liverpool end of month	Thousand boxes			25	21	15
Lard, refined, Liverpool, end of month...	Thousand pounds			6,792	7,284	11,458
rices at Liverpool -	Dollars per 100 lbs.					
Wiltshire sides (Amer.)	"			13.71	20.79	22.35
Wiltshire sides (Can.)	"	14.64	15.01	16.66	22.72	24.14
Wiltshire sides (Dan.)	"	15.60	15.84	21.48	26.49	26.69
Lard, Prime Steam Western	"	11.80	11.86	12.27	17.37	18.89
mark:						
roduction -						
Pigs killed in export slaughter houses.....	Thousands	214	203	323		
rade -						
Exports of bacon	Thousand pounds	23,805	21,861	35,111	23,818	
many:						
roduction -						
Receipt of hogs at 14 cities	Thousands	308	284	233	210	210
Slaughter of hogs at 36 centers	"	369	344	247	273	258

a/ 1911 - 1914 average. b/ Includes Irish Free State. c/ 1913.

Continued

HOGS AND PORK PRODUCTS: INDICES OF FOREIGN SUPPLIES, DEMAND AND PRICE,
CONTINUED

Country and Item	Unit	May 1909-13: Average	June 1909-13: Average	June 1924	May 1925
Germany, continued:					
Trade -					
Imports -	Thousand				
Bacon	pounds	201:	150:	2,357:	875:
Lard	"	16,079:	14,717:	15,305:	13,051:
Exports -					
Bacon to Germany, Bel- gium & Netherlands from U. S. a/	"	908:	775:	959:	1,338:
Lard to Germany, Bel- gium & Netherlands from U. S.	"	15,722:	15,349:	20,606:	21,172:
Prices -	:Dollars per:				
Lard, Hamburg	100 lbs.				18.03:
Margarine, Berlin	"			12.10:	13.29:
Hogs, live weight, Berlin	"	10.96:	10.87:	9.96:	13.72:
Potatoes, feeding, Berlin	"	.37:	.37:b/	.26:	.38:c
Barley, feeding, Leipzig	"	1.75:	1.73:	1.66:	2.30:
United States:					
Production -					
Inspected slaughter...	Thousands	2,747:	2,937:	4,288:	3,186:
Trade -					
Exports of bacon, hams and shoulders	Thousand pounds	29,839:	29,210:	44,144:	33,475:
Exports of lard	"	42,312:	39,449:	59,475:	71,135:
Stocks -					
Lard in cold storage end of month	"	125,145:	153,580:	152,520:	138,295:d
Prices -	:Dollars per:				
Hogs, Chicago	100 lbs.	7.81:	7.90:	7.04:	12.06:
Lard,prime steam,Chicago	"	10.68:	10.77:	12.13:	16.50:

a/ Includes Cumberland sides.   b/ Breslau Price, 1924 and 1925.   c/ First t
   weeks only.   d/ Preliminary.

BETTER ECONOMIC SITUATION IN EUROPE

Economic recovery in Europe in the seven years since the close of the World War has been slow. In some years it has been difficult to see any indications of progress. In any one of the former belligerent countries, however, a comparison of conditions in 1925 with those of 1923 and again with 1921 and 1919 will show that real progress has been made.

Progress has been marked by stabilization of currencies, the repairing of actual war damage to industrial and agricultural equipment, the re-establishment of trade relations, the increase in the volume of manufacture, agricultural production and trade turnover, and consequently the better distribution of the social income, making possible improvement in standards of living.

This economic advance, while it has definitely improved the purchasing power of European countries, does not necessarily make for correspondingly better markets for all kinds of agricultural commodities. The bare necessities of life were imported, even in the extremity of post-war depression, and prosperity will not greatly increase the consumption of these commodities. The effects of increased purchasing power will rather be noted in the greater variety of products which can be marketed, and in the demand for better quality rather than increased quantity of staple goods.

The improvement in economic conditions has not been uniform throughout Europe, and different countries have used different methods in the attempt to gain the desired end of economic prosperity. It will therefore be better to discuss conditions in each of the more important countries separately.

United Kingdom

The United Kingdom is the most highly industrialized country of Europe, and to a greater extent than other countries, must depend for its existence upon the exchange of its manufactured products for food and raw materials from abroad. During the World War this interchange of commodities was interrupted. Food and raw materials were imported in even greater quantities, but they were purchased on credit and the industries which manufactured for export were largely diverted to war activities. Since the war it has not been possible to regain all of the export trade that had been lost. Some of the foreign customers had had their purchasing power reduced by the war, and others, particularly the countries of Asia and the Americas, had developed industries of their own during the war or had turned to other sources of supply. To add to the difficulties of British industry, taxation has been unprecedently heavy. In shipbuilding and coal mining particularly, German reparations in kind have also been factors in preventing the return of prosperity.

But while British industry has been seriously depressed since the war with around a million men constantly unemployed, the fiscal policy of the government has been consistently sound and the credit structure of the country remains unimpaired. The currency has now been restored to gold parity, and with the industrial organization and equipment intact, British industry is prepared to respond quickly to any improvement in market conditions.

During the past three months conditions in the United Kingdom have not been encouraging. Trade Union unemployment at the end of June stood at 12.3 per cent, the highest figure since March 1923. This increase was chiefly in coal mining, although some increase in unemployment took place in most of the key industries except tin plate and sheet steel, linen and the glass trades, which showed slight improvements. There have been, however, slight increases in net profits in most industries in the first half of 1925 over the same months of last year, and exports have shown a very slight increase in the same period. Bank deposits and financial indices have shown little change in recent months.

France

The situation in France is quite the reverse of that in the United Kingdom, in that industry has remained prosperous and employment conditions are, and have been satisfactory. France also in contrast to England, has not attempted until recently to meet current expenses out of revenues. The currency has been repeatedly inflated and exchange has fallen until the franc is worth less than one fourth of par. The interest bearing national debt has been increased rather than diminished. Military employment, together with reconstruction work in the devastated areas, accounts for much of the difference in employment conditions between England and France. With a coal deficit and a less important shipbuilding industry, France is benefitted rather than injured by reparations in kind. With a larger agricultural population and depending less than England upon foreign markets or foreign raw materials, France has not been so seriously injured by the industrial development in America and Asia.

Under these conditions, France is more prosperous in many respects than the United Kingdom, and while its capital equipment is impaired and its credit structure weakened, France is apparently making good progress, and in the absence of further catastrophes will probably show even more rapid gains in the near future.

Germany

There has been a distinct improvement in the German economic situation, beginning with the stabilization of the currency late in 1923. During the past year the textile industries, iron and steel, shipbuilding and coal mining have all been at least fairly active. Unemployment has been greatly reduced although in some industries there is more part time employment. Recent reports indicate reductions in employment in the coal mining industry, which appears to have been over developed because of the

BETTER ECONOMIC SITUATION IN EUROPE - CONT'D.

fear of a coal shortage following the loss of the Saar and Upper Sile-
sian mines. Including lignite, the coal production of the present area
of Germany was greater in 1924 than in 1913, with a distinctly smaller
demand.

German industry is still hampered by abnormally high interest
rates and a lack of sufficient new capital. Markets for export products
were entirely lost during the war and must be recovered, if recovered at
all, in the face of intense competition. But in spite of these difficulties the volume of production has increased and exports have increased
although in 1924 and so far in 1925 imports have greatly exceeded exports.

The heavy balance of visible imports has been made possible to a
large extent by the loans to Germany following the acceptance of the
Dawes Plan. The currency stabilization and general rise in earnings,
brought back to the German market certain types of foreign goods which
had not appeared there for many years. For example, imports of Danish
butter appeared in trade reports immediately after stabilization for the
first time since the war, and in six months, more Danish butter was being
imported than in the same months of 1913. At the same time imports of
lard declined. It seems unlikely, however, that the improvement in German purchasing power will continue at as rapid a rate as in the past
eighteen months.

Italy

The economic situation in Italy is very uncertain. On the sur-
face, however, the economic life of the country seems prosperous. The
budget deficit has been reduced in the past year, bank deposits, loans
and discounts have increased and the number of unemployed on May 31 stood
at the lowest point since October 1920. The iron and steel, cement and
textile industries are running to capacity, and good crops have brought
greater prosperity to the country districts. The lira, however, has declined sharply in the past few weeks with corresponding advances in price
indices, and the past year has witnessed a greatly increased balance of
imports due partly at least to increased imports of wheat and cotton.

Other Countries

Conditions in Spain are rather unfavorable as a result of the
Moroccan war and the poor harvests of 1924. In the minor countries of
Central Europe definite progress in varying degrees has been made during
the past year.

BETTER ECONOMIC SITUATION IN EUROPE - CONT'D.

Of these countries, Poland seems to have made the most progress toward econ
ic stability in recent months. Czechoslovakia has recently imposed a new sc
ule of duties on agricultural products which, however, will not apply to gr
at present prices, but which will automatically become applicable if prices
fall below a certain figure. In Belgium conditions are not very satisfacto.
The industrial organization of Belgium is basically similar to that of Engl
but the fiscal policy of the Belgian government since the war has been simi
to that of the French government. With more limited resources and with sma
domestic markets than France, the consequences of inflation and increasing
debtedness may in the end be more serious. Recently coal reparations deliv
ies from Germany have increased the coal crisis due to over production and i
cumulation of stocks.

In the Netherlands a severe depression followed the superficial pros
perity of war years, but recently there has been increasing stability and
greater prosperity. In Denmark labor troubles have recently interfered witl
foreign trade. On the whole, however, Denmark is prosperous. In Sweden the
iron and steel industry is depressed, but exports of iron ore and wood pulp
have been exceptionally heavy.

Markets for American Exports

Wherever the economic situation improves there should be a better de
mand for American cotton. The larger supplies of cotton during the past ye;
found ready markets at a good price. During the past year large supplies o;
cotton found ready markets at good prices, showing that the demand was stro;
than in 1920-21 and 1921-22 when much lower prices were paid for smaller su;
plies. The market for wheat and flour will depend largely upon the amount
available in each country. Wheat and flour purchases appear to have compar;
tively little relation to economic conditions. The same may be said of fee
ing grains and oil cake. As far as feedstuffs are concerned it seems likel
that Russia will be an increasingly important source of supply. Improved e
nomic conditions seem likely to increase the demand for beef, fresh pork an
the better grades of bacon. The demand for lard in Germany has apparently
declined.

With increasing prosperity in Europe there seems to be a tendency to
ward imposing higher tariffs and more trade restrictions. Italy and Czecho
slovakia have published new tariff schedules on agricultural products, Fran
is again enforcing the embargo against American fresh pork, and Germany is
considering a protective tariff on agricultural products. There is in ever
country a desire to become self-sufficient in foodstuffs, but for the more
highly industrialized countries agricultural self-sufficiency, if possible
all, could only be attained with heavy production costs, which the industri
consumers would be unwilling to bear. Since agricultural unit costs are al
ready high in these countries, no great increases in European crop producti
are expected and no great changes in European demand for agricultural produ
are anticipated.

PORTO RICO EXPECTS TO SHIP MORE GRAPEFRUIT AND PINEAPPLES

Shipments of Porto Rico grapefruit for the year ending June 30, 1926 are expected to exceed the 580,000 boxes sent out during the preceding twelve months, according to H. C. Henricksen, of the Porto Rico Experiment Station. Pineapples are also expected to exceed the 343,000 boxes shipped last year.

Grapefruit bloomed heavily during June and July and a large percentage of the fruit has set. With favorable weather, therefore, and with prices ranging between $4.00 and $5.00 per box, shipments for the period May 1 - November 1, 1925 should be fully 150,000 boxes. Midseason shipments (November 1 to January 1) should reach 400,000 to 500,000 boxes. Excessive rainy weather, however, and lowered prices resulting from heavy supplies from other sources would materially reduce those figures. It is pointed out that 1924-25 shipments would have been much larger had mid-season prices been better, and much smaller had the late season prices not been so extraordinarily good.

PORTO RICO: Number of Grapefruit trees,
1910, 1920, 1925

Type of trees	1910	1920	1925
	Number	Number	Number
Of bearing age	113,000	215,000	220,000
Not of Bearing age	115,000	111,000	50,000

Areas covered are those included in the Census report of 1920.

Pineapple shipments for the year ending June 30, 1926 will be well over the 343,000 boxes shipped during the fiscal year just closed, and may reach 450,000 boxes, according to Mr. Henricksen. Plantings have increased annually during the last few years, and are expected to continue. As with grapefruit, the shipping of pineapples depends very largely upon price conditions in consuming centers. If prices are low, the Porto Rican canneries may take about $\frac{1}{4}$ of the expected 450,000 boxes.

PORTO RICO EXPECTS TO SHIP MORE GRAPEFRUIT AND PINEAPPLES, CONT'D.

PORTO RICO: Number of Pineapple plants,
1910, 1920, 1925

Type of Plant	1910	1920	1925
	Number	Number	Number
Second crop........	15,200,000	7,000,000	7,000,000
First crop.........	9,000,000	2,000,000	8,430,000
To be set in 1925-26.....			8,000,000 to 9,000,000

Areas covered are those included in the Census Report of
1920.

Oranges are not cultivated in groves in Porto Rico. The trees arc
scattered, largely in the mountains. Export figures, therefore, are the best
guide to the trend of production available, although in seasons of low prices
exports do not reflect production accurately.

PORTO RICO: Shipments of Grapefruit, Pineapples
and Oranges, Years ending June 30, 1910 to 1925

Year ending June 30	Grapefruit		Oranges		Pineapples	
	Boxes	Value (dollars)	Boxes	Value (dollars)	Boxes	Value (dollar:
1910......	48,441	162,749	296,058	582,716	277,058	555,0
1911......	96,189	309,698	349,442	703,969	335,641	641,2
1912......	118,937	525,048	277,423	584,414	319,096	684,7
1913......	216,247	726,811	353,690	740,091	360,288	1,142,3
1914......	206,200	751,769	348,927	752,180	369,952	1,246,0
1915......	276,583	834,440	200,311	378,181	552,085	1,723,8
1916......	296,645	837,014	404,451	790,797	532,259	1,176,4
1917......	435,890	939,677	503,318	1,009,737	416,550	916,4
1918......	549,125	1,120,330	603,226	1,231,551	145,605	617,4
1919......	417,369	739,106	373,679	770,303	116,000	458,6
1920......	419,629	1,332,742	336,625	833,575	140,906	479,4
1921......	667,637	2,019,557	162,395	445,986	172,880	574,6
1922......	360,530	1,100,727	388,882	923,912	190,000	600,4
1923......	460,951	1,382,350	732,973	1,449,378	236,605	726,0
1924......	666,657	1,998,869	192,363	471,416	270,317	811,9
1925......	579,736	1,756,015	336,761	838,062	342,547	1,045,9

CHINA MAY HAVE MORE PEANUTS FOR EXPORT

Estimates place peanut production for the 1925-26 season between 70,000 and 80,000 long tons in the Tientsin Consular District, embracing areas which make Tientsin the leading Chinese port of export for unshelled peanuts. Production for the season closed June 30, 1925, is estimated at 50,000 long tons, according to a special report to the Department of Agriculture from Granville Woodard, American Vice Consul at Tientsin. Exports for 1925-26 are estimated at from 15,000 to 20,000 long tons, contingent upon growing conditions. Exports of unshelled peanuts for 9 months of the 1924-25 season ran to 8,600 long tons against 26,000 long tons for the preceding twelve months. Prices in 1924-25 ranged higher than usual, with an easier condition seen for 1925-26.

For the calendar years 1922 and 1923, China exported 27,000 and 52,000 long tons respectively of shelled peanuts. Of the total shipments, 35.7 per cent in 1922 and 34.7 per cent in 1923 were made from Tientsin. The bulk of Chinese peanut exports, however, are made as shelled nuts, in which Tientsin has only a minor share. For the calendar years 1922 and 1923, total exports from China of shelled nuts amounted to 178,000 and 295,000 long tons respectively, about 50 per cent going out at the port of Tsingtao, according to the Chinese Maritime Customs.

Normal movements of peanuts through Tientsin were disturbed in 1924-25 by civil war and the consequent hindrance of transportation. October, November and December are usually the peak months in peanut movements through Tientsin. In 1924, however many tons were diverted to other ports, although included in the Tientsin export figures. While the 1924 crop was smaller than that of 1923, the quality is said to have been maintained. Civil strife delayed the shipping season materially and made interior dealers reluctant to assume the risks incident to moving supplies except at price levels somewhat higher than those of 1923. While the Chinese Ministry of Agriculture has made some effort at experimental improvement of peanuts, no significant advances in crop areas or yields are reported.

Expansion of the oilseed crushing industry of the Netherlands resulted in that country being the largest overseas customer for Tientsin unshelled peanuts in 1924-25. Great Britain held first place the preceding year, with the Netherlands second. Europe generally buys the bulk of the Tientsin exports, the United States taking a comparatively small percentage - 3.2 per cent in 1923-24 and 1.5 per cent in 1922-23. Prices of unshelled nuts in June 1925 were quoted around $5.50 per 100 pounds c.i.f. Pacific ports, of which about 40 cents represented carrying changes. It is felt, however, that the 1925 autumn prices will open at appreciably lower levels.

WOOL PRODUCTION, CONSUMPTION and CLASSIFICATION IN URUGUAY

Production statistics for wool in Uruguay are not availabe but exports during 1924 amounted to approximately 99,000,000 pounds according to a report received from the American Consul, Gaylord Marsh, at Montevideo. Exports during 1923 amounted to approximately 100,000,000 pounds. Germany, England, France, Belgium, the United States and Italy are the most important foreign markets.

A recent official statement, issued by the Ministry of Industries of Uruguay, estimates the annual consumption of wool in that country to be between 7,500,000 pounds and 8,500,000 pounds. The local uses of wool are mainly in the manufacture of woolen fabrics, mattresses, cushions, rugs and saddle blankets.

In view of the comparatively large production of wool in Uruguay and in connection with efforts now being made to bring about a uniform international grading of wool, the classification used in the local markets of Uruguay becomes of interest. The following classification is used by the government, by producers and by dealers up to the time of participation by American and European buyers, when the standards of the purchasers are applied.

URUGUAYAN CLASSIFICATION OF WOOL.

MERINOS

   SUPRAS. Wool that is clean, showy, bright, well grown, of
           strong staple, and of good color and light shrinkage.

   PRIMAS (Firsts). Wool that is not as showy as SUPRAS, but
           bright and well grown like SUPRAS.

   SEGUNDA ENVELLONADA (Seconds in fleeces). High grade, clean
           and of good condition. Like SUPRAS and PRIMAS, this
           type of wool is regraded into four classes: namely,
           BUENAS (Good), REGULARES (Regular), BAJAS (Low),
           and DEFECTUOSAS (Defectives).

   SUELTAS (Wool not in fleeces). Superior quality, well grown,
           clean, and grading according to section for which
           wool comes. Treated as per above classifications.

   DE CORDERO (Lambs' wool). Long staple, and clean of seedy
           wool, or wool containing other vegetable matter.
           RAPON (very short staple).

   BARRIGAS (Belly wool). Graded according to class and condition,
           but free of dung or excessive dirt.

WOOL PRODUCTION, CONSUMPTION, and CLASSIFICATION IN URUGUAY, CONT'D.

LANAS CRUZAS. (Crossbred sheep)

CRUZAS FINAS (Fine crossbreds).
      1.- Supra in quality and free from seeds or burs.
      2.- Good to supra in quality, free from seeds or burs.
      3.- General to good in quality, free from seeds or burs.
      4.- Regular in quality, with occasional burs.
      5.- Inferior in quality, of heavy shrinkage, poorly
         grown, poor color and other defects which make it
         look unattractive.
      6.- Wool that is very seedy and burry, regardless of
         its other good qualities.

CRUZAS MEDIANAS FINAS (Medium fine crossbreds).
      Graded in the six classes mentioned above.

CRUZAS MEDIANAS GRUESAS (Medium coarse crossbreds).
      Graded in the six classes mentioned above.

CRUZAS GRUESAS (Coarse crossbreds).
      Graded in the six classes mentioned above.

CORDEROS (Lambs' wool)
      1.- Graded according to class and length of staple
         and freedom from seeds, burs, and other vegetable
         matter.
      2.- Graded for excessive amount of seeds and burs.
      3.- Graded for its very short staple.

BARRIGAS CRUZAS FINAS (Fine crossbred belly wool).
      1.- Graded according to fineness.
      2.- Graded for tail wool and defective wool.

- - - - - - - -

SISAL IN PORTUGUESE EAST AFRICA

The greater part of sisal in Portuguese East Africa is produced in the
si Valley and its vicinity, and practically the entire production is in
ands of five companies, four of which are operating in the territory
ned by the colonial government, according to Consul Cross at tourenco
es.

Opportunities for sisal production in Portuguese East Africa appear
attractive as the soil and climate have been proved to be splendidly
ed for its growth, labor is abundant and cheap and necessary land suit-
for its cultivation exists in almost unlimited quantities, even close to
existing means of transport.

BRITAIN WOULD IMPROVE FLAX INDUSTRY

The decline of British flax areas since 1920 has stimulated the Committee on Flax Seed and Flax Growing into proposals for rehabilitating the industry. Flax areas over a series of years are presented below:

a/

FLAX: Area in England, Scotland and Wales 1868 to 1924

Year	:	Total	:	Year	:	Total
1868	:	17,543	:	1918	:	19,742
1869	:	20,963	:	1919	:	19,461
1870	:	23,957	:	1920	:	23,917
1871	:	17,366	:	1921	:	8,300
1881	:	6,534	:	1922	:	9,650
1891	:	1,801	:	1923	:	10,054
1901	:	640	:	1924	:	5,869
1911	:	449	:		:	

a/ The flax acreage of Scotland is but a small proportion of the total amounting at the pre-war maximum in 1870 to only about 1,000 acres and at the post war maximum in 1920 to 1,600 acres.

The Committee proposes to have growers concentrate on production Retting and deseeding would be done by a special factory organization under the direction of the Ministry of Agriculture. The project would require about $200,000 during the next two years.

The stoppage by the war of Russian and Belgian supplies of both sowing seed and fiber called for an immediate extension of the flax area in England particularly since the small supplies raised in Ireland were dependent upon imported seed. In the autumn of 1917 the Flax Control Board asked for an immediate extension of flax production in England from the 500 acres then being devoted to that crop to at least 10,000 acres in 1918 in order to provide seed for sowing in Ireland and to provide additional fiber for the manufacture of areoplane cloth. The war boom led to the belief that the flax industry had been established on a permanent basis in England. A slump in the linen trade, however, made it impossible to conduct profitably the various factories which in 1920 were passing or had already passed into private ownership. Out of 12 factories established by the Government during the war only one is now operating.

In the 10 years immediately preceding the war (1903-12) the total imports of raw flax into the United Kingdom averaged 82,496 short tons annually and of tow 19,589 short tons annually. The largest imports since the war were in 1922 when 34,797 short tons of raw flax were imported and 9,535 short tons of tow. Russia and Belgium are the two most important sources of supply. Domestic supplies are derived almost wholly from Ireland; before the war they amounted to from 12,000 to 17,000 tons of flax and tow annually. In 1923 Irish production amounted to only 9,500 tons. There is a small export of raw flax and tow.

EXPANSION OF TRADE IN FRENCH WALNUTS

Exports of shelled and unshelled walnuts from Bordeaux to the United States are increasing, according to W. H. McKinney, American Consul at that port. As much as 80 per cent of American walnut imports come from France, about half of them passing through Bordeaux. Great Britain is the other large consumer of French walnuts, taking about twice as many as does the United States.

FRANCE: Exports to the United States of Walnuts,
Shelled and Unshelled from Bordeaux,
1920 to 1924.

Type	1920	1921	1922	1923	1924
	1,000 pounds	1,000 pounds	1,000 pounds	1,000 pounds	1,000 pounds
Shelled ....:	6,811	8,538	8,144	10,628	11,695
Unshelled ....:	949	3,339	3,226	3,028	3,627
Total ....:	7,760	11,877	11,370	13,716	15,322

Exports were greater for 1924 than for any other postwar year. Prices were higher likewise, going as high as 34 cents per pound, c.i.f. New York. Both prices and shipments have declined since January 1925. Production of French walnuts for the years 1918 to 1922 averaged 88 million pounds. It is said that should demand increase, more walnuts could be made available from the present number of trees. Oil is pressed from those nuts not used as table nuts.

While 1924 is viewed as having been exceptional in the amount of business done and in the high prices obtained in France, it is said that comparatively small profits accrued to French shippers, owing to the high prices asked by French producers and to the sharp competition among exporters for American business. It is suggested further that closer cooperation between American importers and French exporters would result in eliminating many unfavorable conditions now prevalent in the trade. It is said that purchasers should scrutinize more carefully the quality of the goods for which they are bidding, in an effort to encourage a higher standard for the walnuts entering into the export trade. Price fluctuations, while they appear to exhibit little influence upon the total volume of walnuts exported are said to so disorganize the trade as to increase speculation and the consequent feeling of uncertainty in both the terms of the agreement made and in the quality of the goods contracted for.

GRAINS: Exports from the United States, July 1-Aug. 1, 1924 and 1925
PORK:. Exports from the United States, Jan. 1-Aug. 1, 1925

Commodity	: July 1 - : July 31, : 1924	: July 1 - : Aug. 1, : 1925	Week ending		August 1925
			: July 18,: July 25, :		
			: 1925 :	1925 :	
	: 1,000 : bushels	: 1,000 : bushels	: 1,000 : bushels	: 1,000 : bushels	: 1,000 : bushels
GRAINS:	:	:	:	:	:
Wheat .... :	4,049:	5,948:a/	846:a/	964:a/	1,
Wheat flour b/ ..... ;	789:	--- :	--- :	--- :	--
Rye .... :	1,306:	3,884:	515:	294:	
Corn .... :	506:	703:	80:	138:	
Oats .... :	19:	3,231:	491:	401:	
Barley .... :	1,054:	3,004:	1,398:	596 :	
	:	:	:	:	
	:	:January 1-: :August 1 : 1925 c/ :	:	:	
PORK:	:	: 1,000 : pounds	1,000 : pounds :	1,000 : pounds :	1,000 pounds
Hams & shoulders,inc.:	:	:	:	:	
Wiltshire sides ... :	:	173,407:	2,812:	2,704:	2,
Bacon, including	:	:	:	:	
Cumberland sides... :	:	126,641:	2,597:	3,961:	4,
Lard .... :	:	423,068:	· 5,756:	8,848:	6,
Pickled pork .... :	:	14,258:	217:	301:	
	:	:	:	:	

Compiled from official records of the Bureau of Foreign and Domestic Commerc
a/ Including wheat flour via Pacific ports.
b/ Not yet available.
c/ Revised to June 30, including exports from all ports.

- - - - - - - - - - - - - -

BRITISH EXPANDING COTTON PRODUCTION IN KASSALA

An increased cotton crop in Kassala, Anglo-Egyptian Sudan, is anticipated in 1925-26, as a result of the completion of two new canals at
Magauda and Metateib, according to the chairman of the Kassala Cotton Co:
pany, Ltd. In the past season, he states, about 16,000 acres were in cu
tivation and production amounted to 5,900 bales of 478 pounds net. The
crop for Gezira, Kassala and Tokar together, has been fori cast at 22,180
bales according to the International Institute of Agriculture.

Picking in Kassala is now at an end. The variety of cotton grown
principally is Sakellaridis, grading generally somewhat better than "Ful
Good Fair."

BUTTER: Prices in London, Copenhagen and New York
(By Weekly Cable)

Market and Item	July 24, 1925	July 31, 1925	August 7, 1925
	Cents per lb.	Cents per lb.	Cents per lb.
...agen, official quotation a/	42.34	42.72	43.50
...rk, 92 score .... a/	43.50	43.00	43.50
1:			
.sh	43.19	44.24	44.85
:h, unsalted	42.97	43.81	44.85
3h	42.53	42.72	b/
3h, unsalted	43.19	43.15	b/
Zealand	42.32	42.39	42.49
Zealand, unsalted..........	42.97	42.94	42.92
tralian	41.23	41.31	41.62
tralian, unsalted	41.67	41.85	42.06
entine, unsalted	39.06 - 39.93	39.46 - 40.77	40.10
erian	37.32 - 39.06	37.95 - 39.03	38.59
adian	41.01	40.55	41.40
adian, unsalted	b/	41.20	42.28

tions converted at exchange of the day. a/ Thursday price. b/ Not quoted.

EUROPEAN LIVESTOCK AND MEAT MARKETS
(By Weekly Cable)

Market and Item	Unit	Week ending		
		July 22	July 29	August 5
NY:				
eipts of hogs, 14 markets ..	Number	44,195	34,896	52,527
ces of hogs, Berlin	$ per 100 lbs.	16.96	18.36	18.04
ces of lard, tcs., Hamburg..	"	19.82	20.57	20.00
ces of margarine, Berlin ...	"	13.94	13.94	13.94
D KINGDOM AND IRELAND:				
s, certain markets, England.	Number	9,353	9,568	6,740
s, purchases, Ireland	"	13,700	14,286	
ces at Liverpool:				
merican Wiltshires	$ per 100 lbs.	- - -	- - -	- - -
anadian "	"	23.00	23.42	23.83
anish "	"	24.74	25.59	26.22
orts, Great Britain: a/ b/				
utton, frozen	Carcasses	153,570	49,951	
amb, "	"	285,282	93,919	
eef, "	Quarters	94,557	86,204	
eef, chilled	"	129,002	93,059	
RK:				
orts of bacon a/ c/.........	100 lbs.	7,392		

Received through the Department of Commerce. b/ Week ending Saturday
wing date indicated. c/ Week ending Friday following date indicated.

Foreign Crops and Markets   Vol. 11, N.

GRAINS: Exports from the United States, July 1-Aug. 1, 1924 and 1925
PORK: Exports from the United States, Jan. 1-Aug. 1, 1925

Commodity	July 1 - July 31, 1924	July 1 - Aug. 1, 1925	Week ending		
			July 18, 1925	July 25, 1925	Augu 19
	1,000 bushels	1,000 bushels	1,000 bushels	1,000 bushels	1,0 bush
GRAINS:					
Wheat	4,049:	5,948:a/	846:a/	964:a/	
Wheat flour b/	789:	--- :	--- :	--- :	
Rye	1,306:	3,884:	515:	294:	
Corn	506:	703:	80:	138:	
Oats	19:	3,231:	491:	401:	
Barley	1,054:	3,004:	1,398:	596:	
		January 1- August 1 1925 c/			
		1,000 pounds	1,000 pounds	1,000 pounds	1, pou
PORK:					
Hams & shoulders,inc.					
Wiltshire sides ...		173,407:	2,812:	2,704:	
Bacon, including					
Cumberland sides...		126,641:	2,597:	3,961:	
Lard		423,068:	5,756:	8,848:	
Pickled pork		14,258:	217:	301:	

Compiled from official records of the Bureau of Foreign and Domestic Comme
a/ Including wheat flour via Pacific ports.
b/ Not yet available.
c/ Revised to June 30, including exports from all ports.

- - - - - - - - - - - -

BRITISH EXPANDING COTTON PRODUCTION IN KASSALA

        An increased cotton crop in Kassala, Anglo-Egyptian Sudan, is a
ticipated in 1925-26, as a result of the completion of two new canals
Magauda and Metateib, according to the chairman of the Kassala Cotton
pany, Ltd. In the past season, he states, about 16,000 acres were in
tivation and production amounted to 5,900 bales of 478 pounds net. Th
crop for Gezira, Kassala and Tokar together, has been for cast at 22,1
bales according to the International Institute of Agriculture.

        Picking in Kassala is now at an end. The variety of cotton gro
principally is Sakellaridis, grading generally somewhat better than "F
Good Fair."

BUTTER: Prices in London, Copenhagen and New York
(By Weekly Cable)

Market and Item	July 24, 1925	July 31, 1925	August 7, 1925
	Cents per lb.	Cents per lb.	Cents per lb.
Copenhagen, official quotation a/	42.34	42.72	43.50
New York, 92 score .... a/	43.50	43.00	43.50
London:			
Danish	43.19	44.24	44.85
Dutch, unsalted	42.97	43.81	44.85
Irish	42.53	42.72	b/
Irish, unsalted	43.19	43.15	b/
New Zealand	42.32	42.39	42.49
New Zealand, unsalted..........	42.97	42.94	42.92
Australian	41.23	41.31	41.62
Australian, unsalted	41.67	41.85	42.06
Argentine, unsalted	39.06 - 39.93	39.46 - 40.77	40.10
Siberian	37.32 - 39.06	37.95 - 39.03	38.59
Canadian	41.01	40.55	41.40
Canadian, unsalted	b/	41.20	42.28

Quotations converted at exchange of the day.   a/ Thursday price.   b/ Not quoted.

EUROPEAN LIVESTOCK AND MEAT MARKETS
(By Weekly Cable)

Market and Item	Unit	Week ending July 22	July 29	August 5
GERMANY:				
Receipts of hogs, 14 markets ..	Number	44,195	34,896	52,527
Prices of hogs, Berlin	$ per 100 lbs.	16.96	18.36	18.04
Prices of lard, tcs., Hamburg..	"	19.82	20.57	20.00
Prices of margarine, Berlin ...	"	13.94	13.94	13.94
UNITED KINGDOM AND IRELAND:				
Hogs, certain markets, England.	Number	9,353	9,568	6,740
Hogs, purchases, Ireland	"	13,700	14,286	
Prices at Liverpool:				
American Wiltshires	$ per 100 lbs.	- - -	- - -	- - -
Canadian "	"	23.00	23.42	23.83
Danish "	"	24.74	25.59	26.22
Imports, Great Britain: a/ b/				
Mutton, frozen	Carcasses	153,570	49,951	
Lamb, "	"	285,282	93,919	
Beef, "	Quarters	94,557	86,204	
Beef, chilled	"	129,002	93,059	
DENMARK:				
Exports of bacon a/ c/.........	100 lbs.	7,392		

a/ Received through the Department of Commerce.   b/ Week ending Saturday
following date indicated.   c/ Week ending Friday following date indicated.

Index

CPSIA information can be obtained
at www.ICGtesting.com
Printed in the USA
BVHW091737021118
531990BV00019B/1033/P